A Kid's Guide to Drawing the Countries of the World™

How to Draw
Poland's
Sights and Symbols

Melody S. Mis

The Rosen Publishing Group's
PowerKids Press™
New York

To my father, Joseph J. Mis, and his proud Polish family

Published in 2004 by The Rosen Publishing Group, Inc.
29 East 21st Street, New York, NY 10010

First Edition

Editor: Jannell Khu
Book Design: Kim Sonsky
Layout Design: Emily Muschinske

Illustration Credits: Cover and inside by Mike Donnellan.
Photo Credits: Cover and title page (hand) © Arlan Dean; p. 5 © Historical Picture Archive/CORBIS; pp. 9, 24, 34, 38 © Paul Almasy/CORBIS; p. 10 © Larry Lee Photography/CORBIS; p. 13, *Self Portrait*, pastel on paper, 35 x 35 cm, 1902: Muzeum Narodowa Warsaw, Poland / Bridgeman Art Library; p. 14 *Winter Landscape/View from Kosciuszko Mound*, pastel on paper, 91.8 x 60.2 cm, 1905: National Museum in Cracow, Poland / Bridgeman Art Library; p. 16 (bottom) © Adriana Skura; p. 18 © Colin Garratt, Milepost 92/Corbis; p. 20 © Francesc Muntada/Corbis; p. 22, 42 © Dave G. Houser/Corbis; p. 26 © B.C. Biega; p. 28 © Rafal Komierowski; pp. 30, 32 © Carmen Redondo/Corbis; pp. 36, 40 © Hulton-Deutsch Collection/Corbis.

Mis, Melody S.
How to draw Poland's sights and symbols / Melody S. Mis.— 1st ed.
    p. cm. — (A kid's guide to drawing the countries of the world)
Summary: Presents step-by-step directions for drawing the national flag, Wilanow Palace, a corn poppy, and other sights and symbols of Poland. Includes bibliographical references and index.
ISBN 0-8239-6669-0
1. Drawing—Technique—Juvenile literature. 2. Poland—In art—Juvenile literature. [1. Poland—In art. 2. Drawing—Technique.] I. Title. II. Series.
NC655 .M62 2004
743'.936438—dc21

                                    2002153344

Manufactured in the United States of America

CONTENTS

Let's Draw Poland

Twice in its history, Poland did not exist on the map of Europe because it was divided among invading nations. Today Poland is a thriving, independent nation located in the heart of eastern Europe. Poland was settled around 800 A.D. by Slavic peoples who began to move eastward from Europe. In the tenth century, one of the largest Slavic groups in Poland was named Polanie, which means "people who live in the fields." The Polanie gave Poland its name and its first dynasty, called Piast. Poland was founded under the Piasts when King Mieszko I converted to Christianity in 966 A.D., uniting the Slavic groups.

The last Piast king died in 1370. In 1386, the Jagiellonian dynasty came into power. Under the Jagiellonians, Poland was joined with Lithuania to become the largest country in Europe. The Jagiellonian dynasty ended in 1572. During the seventeenth century, Poland was almost destroyed by invading armies from Sweden and Turkey. Jan III Sobieski, who ruled Poland from 1674 to 1696, defeated the

This is a print of the medieval town of Breslau. Today, Breslau is known as Wroclaw and is the fourth-largest city in Poland. "Medieval" has to do with the Middle Ages, the years from A.D. 500 to A.D. 1450.

invaders and reunited Poland. The eighteenth century brought tragedies to Poland. Between 1772 and 1795, Russia, Germany, and Austria invaded Poland and divided Poland among themselves. Poland did not exist again until the end of World War I in 1918, when it became a nation once more. World War II began in 1939, when German Nazis invaded Poland. The Nazis were a group of people in Germany who wanted to get rid of the Jewish race. Many Jews lived in Poland. Under Nazi leader Adolf Hitler, the Nazis built death camps in which they killed more than six million Jews. This mass killing of Jews is called the Holocaust. Located near Kraków, Auschwitz-Birkenau was the largest camp. Today it is a museum dedicated to the people who died there.

When the war ended in 1945, many areas in Poland were destroyed. More than 6.5 million Poles had died from hunger or had been killed. Many of Poland's cities had to be rebuilt. Poland ended up under Communist rule until 1989. In 1980, Poland's economy began to suffer. Many Polish workers protested rising food costs and low wages. In 1980, they formed a union called Solidarity. The union, led by Lech Walesa, went on strike, which means the workers refused to work. The union strikes led to the end of Communism in 1989, and Poland established itself as a democracy.

With this book, you will learn more about Poland and how to draw some of its sights and symbols. You will start with one shape and add other shapes to it. New shapes are shown in red. Directions are printed under each new step. Before you start, you will need the following supplies:

- A sketch pad
- An eraser

- A number 2 pencil
- A pencil sharpener

These are some of the shapes and drawing terms you need to know to draw Poland's sights and symbols:

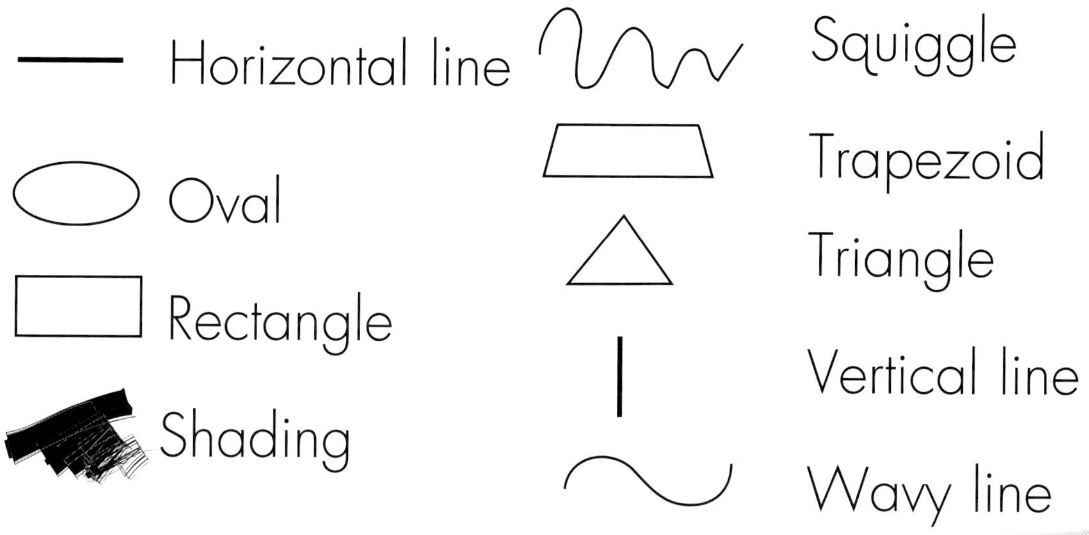

—— Horizontal line

$\sim\!\!\sim$ Squiggle

⬭ Oval

▱ Trapezoid

▭ Rectangle

△ Triangle

▰ Shading

| Vertical line

$\sim$ Wavy line

More About Poland

With an area of 120,728 square miles (312,684.1 sq km), Poland is the second-largest country in central and eastern Europe. Poland is bordered by Russia and the Baltic Sea in the north. Across the Baltic to the northwest lies the country of Sweden. The Sudeten and Tatra Mountains separate southern Poland from the Czech Republic and Slovakia. Poland's eastern neighbors are Lithuania, Belarus, and Ukraine. Germany borders Poland to the west.

More than 38 million people live in Poland, and most of them speak Polish, the national language. The majority of the population are Poles, who are descendants of the Slavs. Some of the minority groups that live in Poland include Ukrainians, who live mainly in the western part of the country, and Belorussians, who live mostly in the eastern section. Before World War II, the Jews were an important minority in Poland. Once, Polish Jews numbered 3.5 million, but today only about 5,000 Jews live in Poland.

This is a view of Warsaw, with the Palace of Culture and Science pictured on the left. This building is Warsaw's tallest building at nearly 850 feet (259 m) tall.

Warsaw is Poland's capital and its most-populated city with 1,615,369 people. It is located in the center of the country near the Vistula River. Łódź, just southwest of Warsaw, has a population of 800,110 and is Poland's second-most-populated city. It is an important textile center. The third-most-populated city is Kraków, with 738,150 residents. Kraków, which served as the nation's capital from 1038 to 1596, is considered Poland's most beautiful city.

Poland's economy is based on agriculture, mining, and industry. Poland's main crops include rye, wheat, potatoes, and sugar beets. The nation has many natural resources that are important to the economy. Poland's mines provide copper, zinc, lead, and one-fourth of the world's coal. Poland's main industries produce chemicals, steel, textiles, glass, and ships. Ever since Christianity was introduced in Poland in the tenth century, the majority of Poles have belonged to the Roman Catholic faith. In 1978, Karol Wojtyla, the former archbishop of Kraków, became the first Pole to be elected leader of the Roman Catholic Church. He is now known as Pope John Paul II.

Kraków is considered one of the most beautiful cities in Europe. Shown here is Zygmunt Chapel, one of the most famous places of worship in Poland.

The Artist Stanislaw Wyspiański

Stanislaw Wyspiański

Stanislaw Wyspiański (1869–1907) was a leading artist of early-twentieth-century Poland. Stanislaw Wyspiański was born in Kraków during the time when Poland was divided between Russia, Germany, and Austria and did not exist as a country. Wyspiański enrolled at Kraków's Academy of Fine Arts in 1887. In 1890, he visited other European countries.

After Wyspiański returned to Poland, he joined a group of artists called Young Poland. These artists worked to spread Polish unity through art. They wanted Poland to be independent from foreign rule. They created art that expressed pride in Poland. The art also showed the country's sad history. Wyspiański depicted this sadness in his art, including many of the stained glass windows he created for several churches in Kraków. Although Wyspiański is best known for his stained glass windows, he is also famous for his pastel drawings. Pastels are special drawing sticks made from colored powders. Using a pastel stick, an artist can apply a stroke of heavy color onto a canvas and smooth it out to make softer shades of that particular color.

Some of Wyspiański's most interesting pastels are drawings, done in 1905, of Kraków's Kościuszko Mound. Wyspiański's *View of Kościuszko Mound* shows the cold winter climate of the mountainous area in southern Poland.

Wyspiański used stark, dull colors to reflect the sadness of the Polish people over the loss of their country.

Wyspiański used pastel on paper to create *View of Kościuszko Mound* in 1905. The drawing measures 36" x 24" (91.4 cm x 61 cm). The mound is a memorial to Tadeusz Kościuszko, a Polish soldier who led an uprising to protest the Russian invasion of Poland during the 1790s.

Map of Poland

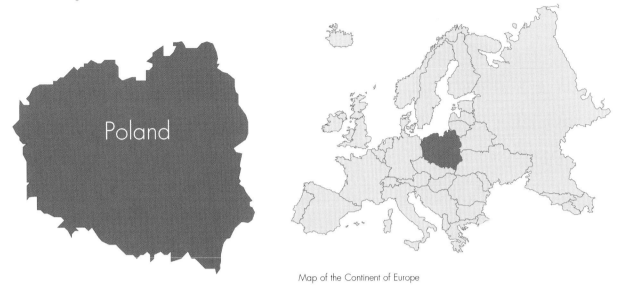

Map of the Continent of Europe

Poland is located in central Europe. Most farms are in the north and the south. In the Pomerania region in the north along the Baltic coast are beaches and sand dunes. This is a popular vacation area. South of the Baltic coast is a chain of lakes surrounded by forests. Many of these forests are nature preserves set aside to protect Europe's largest herd of elk and the smallest forest ponies in the world. Southern Poland is marked by mountains and plateaus. The country's highest point is Rysy Peak, at 8,197 feet (2,498.4 m), in the Tatra Mountains. Poland's southwest region, called Silesia, has Europe's second-largest coal field. Poland's longest river is the Vistula, which is 675 miles (1,086.3 km) long. The Oder river divides Poland from Germany.

1

Start by drawing a large rectangle guide shape. You will erase most guide shapes in this book, so draw them lightly! Next draw a round shape inside the rectangle.

2

You will now draw the shape of Poland inside the round shape. Before you start, look at the map of Poland on the opposite page.

3

Erase the two guide shapes that you drew in step 1. Next draw a small star toward the right. This is Warsaw, the capital of Poland.

4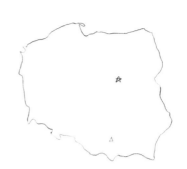

Draw a small triangle on the bottom to show the city Kraków. Some of Poland's sights and symbols that you will learn how to draw are in or near Kraków.

5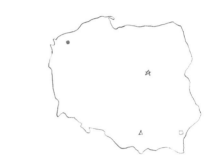

In the top left corner, draw a dot for the region of Pomerania. This is the region where you'll find Malbork Castle, which you'll learn how to draw on page 25. Add a small square to the bottom right to show where Auschwitz is.

6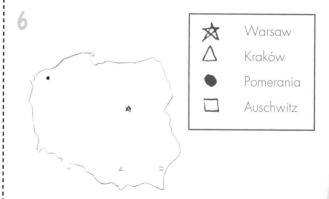

Draw the map key as shown, and you are done.

The Flag of Poland

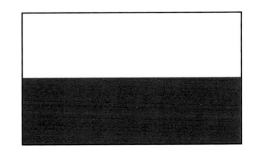

Poland adopted its national flag in 1919. This is the year after Poland became an independent nation. The Polish flag consists of two horizontal stripes that are equal in size. The top stripe is white, and the bottom stripe is red. White stands for peace, and red symbolizes military strength. It is also believed that the white horizontal stripe stands for Poland's emblem, the white eagle. You will learn about the white eagle emblem in the next chapter.

Currency of Poland

The official currency of Poland is the *zloty*, which stands for "gold." Polish coins are stamped with the national emblem, which is the white eagle. "Rzeczpospolita Polska" is written around the coin and is the official name of Poland. The other side of the coin shows how much the coin is worth. Polish banknotes all bear the image of Polish rulers. The banknotes are embossed so that blind people can use them easily.

Flag

1

Begin by drawing a large rectangle.

2

Draw a straight line through the center of the rectangle. Use a ruler if you'd like.

3

Finish by shading the lower half of the rectangle.

Currency

1

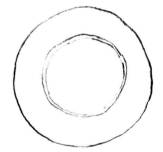

Begin by drawing a large circle with two smaller circles inside.

2

Go to page 19 and follow the step-by-step directions to draw the bird.

3

Add detail inside the bird.

4

Between the border of the two circles, write "RZECZPOSPOLITA POLSKA 1994."

The White Eagle, Emblem of Poland

The white eagle has been the national emblem of Poland for at least 1,000 years. According to legend, it dates from the time of Lech, who was thought to be one of the early founders of Poland. While Lech was riding his horse one day, he spotted a white eagle guarding her babies in her nest. Lech wanted one of the baby birds so that he could train it to hunt other birds and small animals. When he reached for a baby, the mother eagle attacked him. In turn, Lech wounded the mother eagle with his knife. When he saw the red blood from the cut on the eagle's white breast, Lech was ashamed. He decided that he would fight as hard for Poland as the mother eagle had fought for her nest of babies. The white eagle became a symbol of freedom for Poland.

1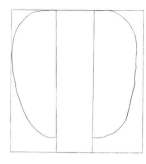

Draw these guide shapes lightly. Draw a square. Draw a vertical rectangle in the center of the square. Draw two half circles on either side of the rectangle.

2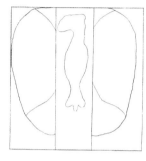

Draw the bird's head, body, and tail using the rectangle guide. For the wings, use the half circle guides to draw four curved lines as shown.

3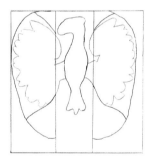

Shape the outer part of the wings with curved lines. Connect the bird's wings to the body with short horizontal lines.

4

Next draw the curved lines shown on its tail.

5

Erase the guide shapes. Draw the shape on the bird's chest. Draw three wavy lines on either side of the tail. Add curved shapes below the tail.

6

Draw one shape at a time. Start with the face. Notice that the face is looking toward the left. Next draw the lines and shapes on the bird's body, tail, and wings. Draw the oval shape that you see on the lower part of its tail. Draw the eagle's legs.

7

The wings are the most detailed part of the drawing, so add many lines and curves to show all the feathers. Notice the three different layers of feathers in each wing.

8

Shade the bird. You are done!

The Corn Poppy

The corn poppy is the national flower of Poland. This flower is one of the world's most popular wildflowers. A wildflower is a flower that grows in fields, gardens, or other places without being planted or tended by people.

The corn poppy grows to be about 2 feet (.6 m) tall. The stem of the corn poppy is unusual, because it has rough, scratchy hairs on it. The flower of the corn poppy is from 2 to 4 inches (5.1–10.2 cm) wide. Its petals are red with black coloring near the stem.

Seeds from the corn poppy are used in baked goods such as cakes, breads, and cookies. They are also ground and made into a cooking oil. The corn poppy is known as the symbol of sleep, because it contains a substance that can make people sleepy.

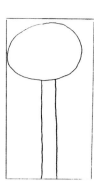

1 To draw the corn poppy, draw a light rectangle guide. Toward the top of the rectangle, draw an oval shape. Next draw a thin rectangle beneath the oval shape. This will be the flower's stem.

4 If you look at the photograph on the opposite page, you'll see that the stem has thin, hairlike growths on it. They grow horizontally from the stem. Start from the top and work your way downward to draw this detail on the stem.

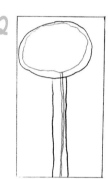

2 Draw the outline of the flower inside the oval. Draw the outline of the stem inside the thin rectangle.

5 To add detail to the inside of the flower, draw some curved lines. Notice that some are lines and others are shapes. Draw one line or shape at a time.

3 Start this step by erasing the guide shapes. Next add two petals, one on the left side and one on the right side. Look at the photograph of the corn poppy on the opposite page for help.

6 Finish the drawing of the corn poppy by shading as shown. Don't shade too darkly, or you'll cover the details you've worked hard to draw.

Jasna Góra Monastery

In 1382, Catholic monks built the Jasna Góra Monastery in the town of Częstochowa. The Jasna Góra Monastery is a huge complex enclosed by walls to protect it from attack. Inside the walls there are several buildings, including a church that contains one of Poland's most treasured icons, the Black Madonna. The Black Madonna is a painting of Mary with the Christ child. It is called the Black Madonna because the color of Mary's face has turned black with age. Some people believe that the Madonna was painted by St. Luke on a piece of wood that was made by St. Joseph. Many Poles pray to the Black Madonna, because they believe she can perform miracles.

1 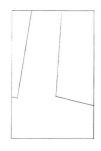 Draw a large rectangle. Inside the rectangle, add four slanted lines. Two lines are mostly horizontal, and two lines slant vertically. Notice the directions in which the lines slant.

2  At the bottom of the rectangle, add three shapes that will be the houses of the monastery. You will first draw the house on the left side. For now you'll just draw two lines. Next draw the center house. It has a rounded roof with a circle on top. Draw a similar house on the right.

3 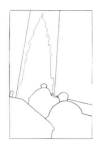 Between the shapes you drew in step 1, draw the tower. It is wide toward the bottom and pointy on the top.

4 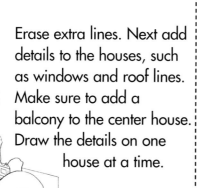 Erase extra lines. Next add details to the houses, such as windows and roof lines. Make sure to add a balcony to the center house. Draw the details on one house at a time.

5 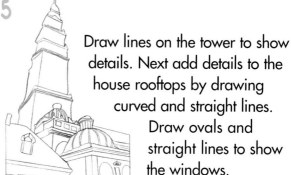 Draw lines on the tower to show details. Next add details to the house rooftops by drawing curved and straight lines. Draw ovals and straight lines to show the windows.

6 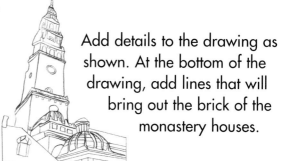 Add details to the drawing as shown. At the bottom of the drawing, add lines that will bring out the brick of the monastery houses.

7 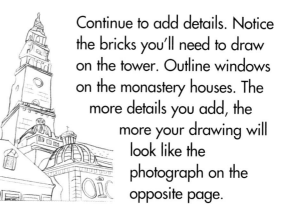 Continue to add details. Notice the bricks you'll need to draw on the tower. Outline windows on the monastery houses. The more details you add, the more your drawing will look like the photograph on the opposite page.

8  Complete your drawing by shading. Shade so that the left side is darker than the right side.

Malbork, the Castle of the Teutonic Knights

Teutonic Knights began to build a castle in the town of Malbork in the thirteenth century. These knights were a German military-religious order that came about from wars called the Crusades. The knights were trained in battle. They became so powerful that they started to take lands from other countries. They captured the Polish town of Malbork and held it for 183 years until the Poles defeated them in 1457. The

Castle of the Teutonic Knights is made of a large monastery, a four-story palace, the Church of Saint Mary, and farm buildings. A moat and high walls surround the castle. The knights watched for approaching enemies from atop these high walls.

1  Draw a large square guide shape. Add two lines on the bottom of the square. Next draw slanted lines. Before you draw, look ahead to the next step to see how these lines will be used.

2  In the lower right corner, draw the curved shape. Shape the castle rooftops by using the lines you drew in step 1. Also look at the photograph on the opposite page for help. Erase extra lines.

3  Draw the triangle shape. Draw the shape left of the triangle. Next add all the lines that you see in red.

4  Draw the set of small buildings on the lower left side. Add two shapes on the right side for trees. Draw a long, thin chimney on the roof. Add lines on the wall and the roof on the right.

5  Erase extra lines. On the right side of the castle, draw a large, wavy shape. This is a guide shape to draw the trees. Next add all the red lines that you see on the roof and towers. Add straight lines at the bottom of the castle.

6  Draw the lines on the rooftops of the castle. Using the tree guide shapes, start drawing the ragged outlines of the trees.

7  Draw the castle's many windows by making small shapes and upside-down U shapes. Erase the guide shapes for the trees.

8  Next you can shade the castle. Draw small X patterns on the left side of the tower. Add detail, such as flags, as shown.

The Mermaid of Warsaw

The mermaid has been a symbol of Warsaw since the fourteenth century. There are many images and statues of mermaids in Warsaw. It was believed that this mythical creature protected Warsaw. One of the earliest images of the Warsaw mermaid shows its upper body to be that of a woman, and its lower body to be that of a sea monster with wings, claws, and a tail. Over the years the mermaid has changed to the half-woman, half-fish image that you will draw in this chapter. The Warsaw mermaid has always been depicted with a sword in one hand and a shield in the other hand to show the fighting spirit of the Polish people. The image of the fighting mermaid is especially symbolic of Warsaw, a city that has been the site of many battles.

1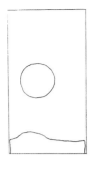

Start by drawing a rectangle. Draw a circle. This is the shield. Next add the shape on the bottom of the rectangle. Notice that it has a roundish hump on the left side. This is the base.

2

Draw the curved lines to connect the two guide shapes to form the body of the mermaid. Notice the shape of her tail. You may find it helpful to look at the other steps as well as the picture on the opposite page.

3

On top of the circle, draw the outline of the face and the arm holding the sword. Draw the mermaid's head, upper back, chest, arm, and sword. Notice that she is facing left.

4

There is an image of a bird inside the shield. First draw another circle inside the shield and then add the shape of the bird as shown.

5

Erase the guide shapes. Go over the mermaid with the lines that you see here. Start from the top and work your way down. You are shaping and adding detail to the mermaid.

6

Draw the scales on the mermaid's tail. Draw the mermaid's face and add details to her hair. Complete this step by adding details on the mermaid's shield.

7

Add more lines to the mermaid's hair. Draw the curvy and wavy lines on the base.

8

Shade your mermaid, and you are done. Don't shade too darkly, or you will cover all the details that you worked hard to draw.

The Cathedral of St. Stanislaw and St. Waclaw

Located in Kraków, the Cathedral of St. Stanislaw and St. Waclaw is one of Poland's most important churches. It is often called the royal cathedral because kings were crowned and were buried there. Built

between 1320 and 1364, the cathedral is dedicated to St. Stanislaw and St. Waclaw. St. Stanislaw was the bishop of Kraków in the eleventh century. He became the patron saint of the city and of Poland. After his death, he was buried in a silver coffin that is on display in the cathedral. St. Waclaw was a tenth-century king of the Czech Republic, southwest of Poland. He was a kind and generous man who was killed for spreading Christianity. Statues of saints decorate one of the cathedral's pointed towers. Poland's largest bell hangs in another tower. The Zygmunt Bell, made in 1520, weighs 12 tons (10.9 t) and is 6 feet (1.8 m) wide.

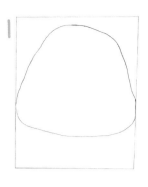

1 Start with a rectangle guide shape. Next draw the shape inside. Notice that this shape is rounded with a wider bottom than top. This is the guide shape of the bell.

2 Inside the guide shape, draw the outline of the bell.

3 Erase the bell guide shapes. Add a small oval to the top of the bell. Draw a large oval at the bottom. This is the bottom opening of the bell.

4 Draw a curved line above the top of the oval you drew in the last step. Inside the opening of the bell, draw a long, thin horizontal rectangle.

5 Add curved lines to the top and the inside oval of the bell. Draw a vertical rectangle that comes out of the bell's opening.

6 Inside the guide rectangle you drew in the last step, draw the outline of the bell ringer. When you have finished with that, add lines around the horizontal rectangle.

7 Erase the vertical rectangle guide shape. Shade as shown. Notice the darker wood grain lines in the bell ringer.

29

The Salt Mine at Wieliczka

The town of Wieliczka, located southeast of Kraków, is famous for its salt mine. Ancient rock salt deposits were discovered there 700 years ago, and they have been mined ever since. The salt mine at Wieliczka is so unusual that it is listed as a World Heritage Site. In the underground mine there are nine levels that reach a total of 442 feet (134.7 m) in depth. There are also about 186 miles (299.3 km) of tunnels. Saltwater lakes, old mining equipment, and sculptures carved by the miners are found in the underground tunnels. Some of the carved sculptures date from the seventeenth century. One of the most impressive features of the

mine is a small church with stairs, an altar, and hanging light fixtures, all carved from salt!

1

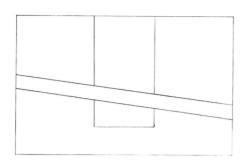

Draw a large rectangle. Draw a smaller rectangle in the center that is broken by a long, thin rectangle. These are guide shapes.

2

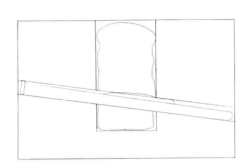

Inside the guide shapes, draw the outline of the salt-mining machine.

3

Erase the guide shapes. Add curved lines in the center. They are ropes. Next draw the four pegs that stick out. Add another curved line at the top.

4

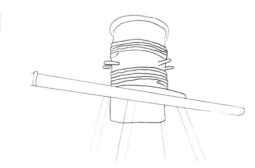

At the bottom of the drawing, add straight lines that will make the bottom supports.

5

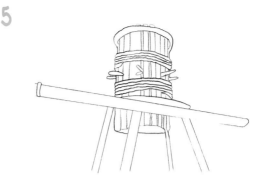

Erase extra lines at the bottom. Next begin drawing vertical lines to show the different wood planks that make up the machine. Draw two more pegs that stick out. Add the three small shapes to the top. Connect the bottoms of the vertical lines.

6

Add small lines on the ropes. Draw a few circles and dots on the wood planks to show the nails. Finish by drawing the small shapes on the bottom of the machine.

7

Shade your drawing, and you are finished.

Warsaw's Royal Castle

The unusual thing about Warsaw's Royal Castle is that most of it was built between 1971 and 1981! The original castle was destroyed during World War II. The castle, which once served as the home of Poland's rulers, was so important to the Poles that they donated money to rebuild it. The original castle was built in the fourteenth century by the Mazovian dukes, who ruled the area around Warsaw.

When Warsaw became the capital of Poland in 1596, the castle was redesigned in the shape of a pentagon. Over the years other buildings, including a palace and a library, were added. One of the most interesting features of the castle is the clock tower, which displays the same clock that was put there in 1622. Today the castle is a museum of Polish history.

1

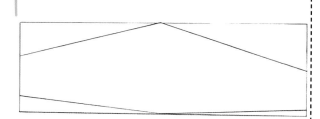

To draw the Royal Castle, start with a long rectangle. Draw two lines that meet up at a point. Draw two lines on the bottom as shown.

2

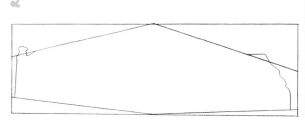

On the ends of the lines, draw the outlines of the sides of the castle as shown.

3

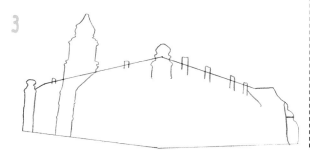

Erase the rectangle guide. Next draw the many shapes along the castle rooftop and at its ends.

4

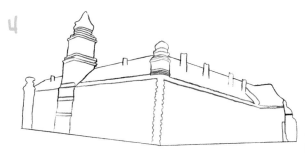

Erase any extra lines on the rooftop. Next draw details on the towers and rooftop. They are mostly horizontal lines. Draw two horizontal lines that almost meet in the middle. Add wavy vertical lines in the center of the drawing. Draw two lines on the bottom right.

5

Start adding small details to the insides of the palace towers, such as rectangles and circles for windows. Draw the tall tower poles. Add further detail to the roof.

6

The castle has many windows. Before you draw them, first draw horizontal lines to separate the floors of the castle. Starting from the first floor, draw rectangular windows. Be patient. Also add the upside-down-*U*-shaped doors. Add many horizontal lines between the two wavy vertical lines.

7

Finish the Royal Castle by shading as shown.

Wilanów Palace

Wilanów is one of Poland's most impressive palaces. Jan III Sobieski purchased Wilanów in 1677. The king wanted a retreat where he could get away from his duties and rest. He hired the royal architect, Augustyn Locci, to turn Wilanów into a baroque palace. Baroque architecture is a style that is characterized by curved lines and ornate decorations. The entrance to Wilanów Palace is through a gate with sculptures on each side. These sculptures symbolize war and peace. The palace is *U* shaped and has two wings that come out from the main building. There are about 60 rooms inside the palace, including a library, a grand hall where musicians entertained guests, and a dining room with a table big enough to seat 50 people. Surrounding the palace are gardens decorated with statues that represent people from history and literature.

1

To draw Wilanów Palace, begin by drawing a long rectangle with another one inside it.

2

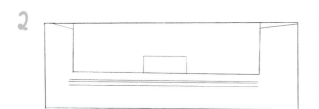

Add several straight lines below the smaller rectangle. Next add three lines in the center of the drawing. Draw two lines in the upper corners.

3

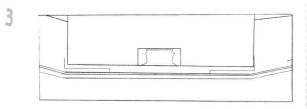

Inside the small rectangle, draw the shape of the palace rooftop. Add more straight lines to the left and the right sides of the rectangle.

4

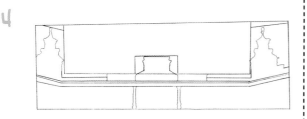

On the left and the right sides, draw the tops of the towers. Notice how the towers are wide at the bottom and narrow toward the top. In the center of the palace, add the two middle columns. Add four small lines in the center.

5

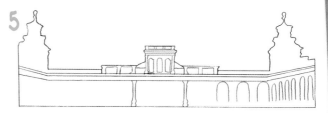

Erase the guide shapes and then start adding the arches inside the palace. Notice that they look like upside-down *U* shapes. Add detail to the top of the palace.

6

Draw the many windows of the palace. Some are squares and some are rectangles. Draw a guide shape on the left. This will help you to draw the trees. Add lines to the two towers on the left and the right sides. Start from the top and work down.

7

Make the ragged outline of the trees within the tree guide. Next add smaller shapes on top of the palace rooftops. Add detail to the windows and towers. Erase extra lines.

8

Shade the trees and towers the darkest and then lightly shade the windows and the arches.

The Chapel of Skulls

One of the oddest attractions in Poland is the Chapel of Skulls. It is located near Kudowa Zdroj in the southwestern part of the country. The chapel is a reminder of Poland's past tragedies. The Chapel of Skulls was built in 1776. It was built by a priest who wanted to store the skulls and bones of soldiers who  died in various wars as well as people who died from outbreaks of diseases, or sicknesses, such as cholera. The chapel priest covered the walls, ceiling, and altar of the chapel with 3,000 skulls and 20,000 bones! There are also thousands of bones tucked away in a crypt. A crypt is an underground room. The remains of the priest who built the chapel are in a glass case that is located near the altar.

1

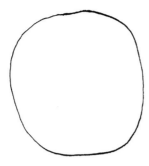

Begin by drawing a circle guide shape.

2

Use the circle guide to draw the shape of the skull. Notice that the bottom of the face is narrower. The bottom is also flat.

3

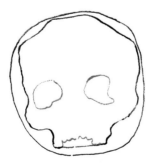

Along the bottom of the skull, draw the outline of the broken teeth. Next draw the eye sockets. Notice that they are not perfectly round. Erase the round guide shape as well as the line underneath the broken teeth.

4

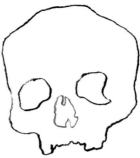

Draw the nose of the skull. This doesn't have to look perfect. Just try to make the nose shape similar to the one shown.

5

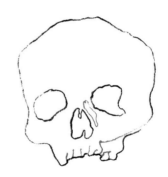

Shape the broken teeth by drawing small lines. Draw the line on the right side of the skull. Next draw the shape between the right eye socket and the nose.

6

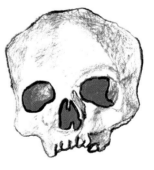

Shade the skull. Begin your shading by making the nose and eye sockets the darkest.

Frédéric François Chopin

Frédéric François Chopin (1810–1849) is one of the world's greatest musical composers. A musical composer writes music. Chopin was born in Zelazowa Wola, near Warsaw. He gave his first public concert at age eight. Before he entered the Warsaw Conservatory in 1826, Chopin had already composed and performed polonaises and mazurkas, which are Polish dances, on the piano. When Chopin was 21 years old, he moved to France. Although Chopin never returned to Poland, he expressed love for his country through his music, especially the polonaises. Poland honored Chopin by erecting a monument of him in Lazienki Park in Warsaw. Sculpted in 1908, it shows Chopin under a willow tree. Concerts of Chopin's music are held by the monument in the summer.

1  Begin by drawing a square guide shape. Next draw a guide shape for Chopin's monument.

2  Use the guide shape to draw the outline of the monument. Notice that the right side has many bumps.

3 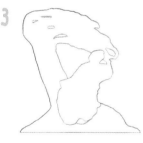 Erase the guide shapes, except for the bottom line. Draw the shape of Chopin. Look at the photograph before you start. Draw the other shapes that you see in red.

4  Add the outlines of Chopin's hair, face, hands, and robe. On the top of the sculpture, add shapes to show the carvings.

5  Add further detail to the sculpture by drawing curved lines throughout to show the folds of the robe and the shapes of the carvings.

6  Add more curved lines, and then draw the details of Chopin's face and hair.

7  Finish by shading your drawing.

39

Maria Skłodowska Curie

Maria Skłodowska Curie (1867–1934) was born in Warsaw. She was very smart and graduated from high school at age 15. After high school, Maria went to study science at the Sorbonne College in Paris, France. There she met and married a scientist named Pierre Curie. At the Sorbonne, Maria received advanced college degrees in mathematics

and physics. In 1903, the Curies won the Nobel Prize for their discovery of radioactivity. Radiation is a process of producing energy. Maria then discovered two elements that produce radioactivity. She named polonium for Poland and named the other element radium. Radium is used today to treat cancer patients. In 1911, Curie won the Nobel Prize again in chemistry for the discovery of these two elements.

1

Draw an oval for Maria Curie's head. Draw a line to shape her face and hairline. Next draw an upside-down *U* guide. Use the guide to shape her body. Draw a line for her collar. Draw another line for the back part of her neck that connects it to her body.

2

Erase the guide shapes. Draw another guide shape on top of her head. This will be used to shape her hair. Draw a slanted line to give her shirt a *V* shape.

3

Inside the guide shape for the hair, draw the outline of the hair. Next move to the face and draw a straight vertical line down the middle and four lines across as shown. These will be used as guides to draw the eyes, nose, and mouth.

4

Erase the hair guide shape. Draw two ovals for the eyes. Add the lips. Draw a larger *V* outline shape outside the first one to show the detail of her jacket. Add a line for her ear.

5

Draw the outline of the nose. Add a horizontal line on her lips. Add lines to the eye area.

6

Erase the face guide. Add the outline of her hair on the left. Add details to the eyes and add an eyebrow. Draw the shape of her nostrils, and add detail to the inner ear. Add lines to the left side of the collar.

7

Add two circles in each eye and a line for her other eyebrow. Add detail to the blouse by drawing little shapes. Add detail to her hair.

8

Shade your drawing. Don't shade the hair too darkly, or you'll cover the details. Notice the dark shading on the shapes on her blouse.

Monument to the Heroes of the Warsaw Uprising

In August 1944, Poland's army rose up against the German Nazis who occupied Warsaw. The Polish army fought the Nazis for two months. Russia's army was supposed to help the Poles, but it did not enter the battle. The Polish army was forced to give up. The uprising was important because it was one of the few times people took a stand against the Nazis. Wincenty Kucma sculpted the bronze monument to the heroes of the Warsaw Uprising. In 1989, it was dedicated to the brave Polish soldiers. It shows some soldiers defending a bunker and other soldiers going down into the sewers, where they could hide from the Nazis and could travel underground in secret.

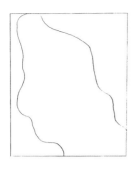

1. Start with a large rectangle. Draw a guide shape in the rectangle. This will be the guide shape that will help you draw the soldier.

2. Use the guide shape to draw the shape of the soldier as shown. Before you start, study the photograph on the opposite page.

3. Erase the guide shapes. Add the shape on the right between the soldier's arm and his body. Draw a line across the top for his helmet. Draw a rectangle and a line for the base.

4. Draw the rifle and part of his hand. Notice that the rifle is slanting upward.

5. Draw the details of the soldier's uniform and long coat. Draw its collar. Draw lines for the belt and cuff. Next add the details to the lower part. The long lines show the folds of his coat. Add a curved line to the gun.

6. Draw the soldier's face by drawing the outline of the soldier's mouth, nose, and chin. Add the trigger to the rifle. Add more details to the uniform using curved lines.

7. Add horizontal lines to the base. Add his eye. Add detail to his hands. Add the finishing touches to the soldier's coat and gun. Erase extra lines.

8. Add shading. Notice that the inner folds of the soldier's coat are the darkest.

Timeline

500s–800s	Slavic tribes settle in Polish territory.
900s	The Polanie unite under the Piast dynasty.
966	Poles adopt Christianity under leadership of Mieszko I.
1079	Bishop Stanislaw is murdered and becomes a martyr.
1200s	The Teutonic Knights settle in northern Poland.
1386	The Jagiellonian dynasty is founded.
1457	The Poles defeat the Teutonic Knights.
1596	The capital of Poland moves from Kraków to Warsaw.
1601	Poland begins a war with Sweden.
1660	The war with Sweden ends.
1683	Jan III Sobieski defeats the Turks at the Battle of Vienna.
1772	Poland is invaded by Russia, Germany, and Austria.
1791	Poland adopts its constitution on May 3.
1795	Poland does not exist on the map of Europe.
1831	Poles rebel against Russia.
1903	Maria Skłodowska Curie receives the Nobel Prize for Physics.
1918	Poland regains independence after World War I.
1939	World War II begins.
1944	The Polish army rises against the Nazis.
1945	World War II ends and Poland is under Communist rule.
1978	Cardinal Karol Wojtyla is elected leader of the Roman Catholic Church.
1980	Trade unions are formed under the banner of Solidarity.
1989	Communist rule ends in Poland.

Poland Fact List

Official Name	Republic of Poland
Area	120,728 square miles (312,684.1 sq km)
Population	38,647,000
Capital	Warsaw
Most Populated City	Warsaw, population 1,615,369
Industries	Chemicals, steel, iron, food products, textiles, machinery
Agriculture	Potatoes, rye, barley, sugar beets, wheat, hogs, cattle
Natural Resources	Coal, copper, salt, lead, zinc
National Emblem	White eagle on a red background
National Dance	The polonaise
Favorite Flower	Corn poppy
Highest Mountain Peak	Rysy Peak, 8,197 feet (2,498.4 m)
Longest River	Vistula, 675 miles (1,086.3 km)
National Language	Polish
National Holiday	Constitution Day, May 3
National Song	"Poland Has Not Yet Succumbed"

Glossary

architect (AR-kih-tekt) Someone who creates ideas and plans for a building.

balcony (BAL-kuh-nee) An upper floor that sticks out over another floor.

bronze (BRONZ) A golden brown blend of copper and tin metals.

cancer (KAN-ser) A sickness in which cells multiply out of control and do not work properly.

characterized (KER-ik-tuh-ryzd) Marked by.

chemistry (KEH-mih-stree) A type of science that deals with the way matter changes.

Christianity (kris-chee-A-nih-tee) A faith based on the teachings of Jesus Christ.

Communist (KOM-yuh-nist) Belonging to a system in which all the land, houses, and factories belong to the government and are shared by everyone.

conservatory (kun-SER-vuh-tor-ee) A school that specializes in one of the fine arts, such as music.

Crusades (kroo-SAYDZ) Wars begun by European Christians who tried to take back the Holy Land from the Muslims in the eleventh through the thirteenth centuries.

culture (KUL-chur) The beliefs, practices, and arts of a group of people.

dedicated (DEH-dih-kayt-ed) Gave to a purpose.

democracy (dih-MAH-kruh-see) A government that is run by the people.

deposits (dih-PAH-zits) Things that are left behind.

descendants (dih-SEN-dents) People born of a certain family or group.

dunes (DOONZ) Hills of sand piled up by the wind.

dynasty (DY-nas-tee) A series of rulers who belong to the same family.

emblem (EM-blum) A picture with a saying on it.

embossed (im-BOSD) Decorated a surface with a picture that is raised.

icons (EYE-konz) Pictures or images that are godly.

independent (in-dih-PEN-dent) Free from the control of others.

industry (IN-dus-tree) A moneymaking business in which many people work and make money producing a particular product.

invading (in-VAYD-ing) Entering a place in order to attack and conquer it.

legend (LEH-jend) A story, passed down, that cannot be proven.

Middle Ages (MIH-dul AY-jez) The period in European history from about A.D. 500 to A.D. 1450.

minority (my-NOR-ih-tee) Having to do with a group of people that is in some way different from the larger part of a population.

miracles (MEER-uh-kulz) Wonderful or unusual events said to have been done by God.

moat (MOHT) A deep ditch, usually filled with water, that keeps people and animals from crossing it.

mythical (MITH-ih-kul) Based on or described in old stories; not real.

Nobel Prize (noh-BEL PRYZ) An award given each year to a person or a group for their work or study.

patron saint (PAY-trun SAYNT) A special saint who is thought to help an individual, a trade, a place, a group, or an activity.

plateaus (pla-TOHZ) Broad, flat, high pieces of land.

protested (PROH-test-ed) Acted on a disagreement.

radioactivity (ray-dee-oh-ak-TIH-vih-tee) The property of certain chemical matter that gives off radiation.

resources (REE-sors-ez) Supplies or sources of energy or useful materials.

rock salt (ROK SOLT) A natural form of the table salt we eat.

sculptures (SKULP-churz) Figures that are carved or formed.

site (SYT) The place where a certain event happens.

substance (SUB-stans) Any matter that takes up space.

symbols (SIM-bulz) Objects or pictures that stand for something else.

textile (TEK-styl) Woven fabric or cloth.

thriving (THRYV-ing) Doing well, growing strong.

tragedies (TRA-jeh-deez) Very sad events.

Index

Web Sites

Due to the changing nature of Internet links, PowerKids Press has developed an online list of Web sites related to the subject of this book. This site is updated regularly. Please use this link to access the list:
www.powerkidslinks.com/kgdc/poland/